Communication with the Dead

STUART A. KALLEN

THE LIBRARY OF
Ghosts & Hauntings

ReferencePoint
Press®

San Diego, CA

ABOUT THE AUTHOR

Stuart A. Kallen is a prolific author who has written more than 250 nonfiction books for children and young adults over the past 20 years. His books have covered countless aspects of human history, culture, and science from the building of the pyramids to the music of the twenty-first century. Some of his recent titles include *How Should the World Respond to Global Warming, Romantic Art,* and *The World Energy Crisis.* Kallen is also an accomplished singer-songwriter and guitarist in San Diego, California.

Picture credits: Cover: iStockphoto.com
Maury Aaseng: 8
AP Images: 20, 35, 37, 41, 47, 60, 62
iStockphoto.com: 55

Landov: 53
North Wind: 5
Photoshot: 10, 15, 23, 26
Science Photo Library: 38, 49

Series design and book layout:
Amy Stirnkorb

LIBRARY OF CONGRESS CATALOGING-IN-PUBLICATION DATA

Kallen, Stuart A., 1955-
  Communication with the dead / by Stuart A. Kallen.
    p. cm. -- (Library of ghosts and hauntings)
  Includes bibliographical references and index.
  ISBN-13: 978-1-60152-089-0 (hardback)
  ISBN-10: 1-60152-089-1 (hardback)
  1. Spiritualism--Juvenile literature. I. Title.
  BF1261.2.K35 2009
  133.9--dc22

                                                    2009009264

Contents

Introduction

Spirits and Spiritualism

The date was April 23, 1863, and a gaunt, bearded man sat at a table with his wife, her sister, and a woman named Nettie Colburn. The parlor was dark, and candles lit the faces of the 4 people who sat with their palms placed on a table. They were taking part in a séance, a gathering held to communicate with the dead. The sitting was led by Colburn, a well known medium who claimed she could convey messages from spirits that existed in the afterlife. After drawing deep, rhythmic breaths to put herself in a trance, Colburn spoke out. She ordered 2 dead boys, Eddie, age 4, and Willie, age 12, to appear and speak to their grieving parents. It is unknown if the dead children obeyed Colburn's commands at that moment, but the mother later told her sister: "Willie lives. He comes to me every night . . . with the same sweet adorable smile he always has had. He does not always come alone. Little Eddie is sometimes with him"[1]

The man in the story was President Abraham Lincoln. The mother of the 2 boys was Lincoln's wife, Mary Todd Lincoln. The first lady suffered severe depression caused by Eddie's death from tuberculosis. Her pain intensified

10 months later when Willie was killed by typhoid fever. After the boys died, Mrs. Lincoln held at least 8 séances in the White House, hoping to be rejoined with the spirits of her sons. And after her husband was assassinated on April 15, 1865, Mrs. Lincoln attended séances for years, trying to contact her murdered husband.

Diffusion of Spiritual Knowledge

Mary Todd Lincoln was among millions of people in the second half of the nineteenth century who became spiritualists—people who sought to communicate with the dead. According to Civil War historian Jean H. Baker, they believed that "after the dead had shed their bodies like a snake's skin, their spirits remained available to those who knew how to contact them."[2] Interest in spiritualism among upper- and middle-class people can be traced back to the 1840s, when the writings of a seventeenth-century Swedish mystic named Emanuel Swedenborg became popular in the United States and Great Britain. Swedenborg believed that trained mediums or perceptive individuals could contact the spirits of the dead. By the 1860s thousands of people had taken up spiritualist beliefs and practices. Journalist Nathanial

Mary Todd Lincoln, wife of President Abraham Lincoln, took part in many séances in hopes of contacting her two young sons, who both died of illness, and her husband, whose life was cut short by an assassin's bullet.

Willis claimed there were 40,000 spiritualists in Boston, which had a population of 177,000. The city had 4 spiritualist newspapers and a large organization called the Society for the Diffusion of Spiritual Knowledge.

By the end of the nineteenth century, the number of spiritualists in the United States and Great Britain had grown to more than 8 million, according to some estimates. The movement remained strong until the 1920s, when widespread publicity about mediums taking advantage of grieving people lessened enthusiasm for spiritualism. The movement was hurt by stories of mediums using trick tables on wires that jumped around the room and assistants dressed in long, flowing robes pretending to be ghosts.

Grief and Belief

Although the spiritualist movement fell out of favor with the public, the idea of talking to the dead remains popular in the twenty-first century. Modern-day mediums (sometimes called psychics or channelers) employ some of the same techniques used by their predecessors. They go into trances and use techniques such as clairvoyance, or "clear seeing," to speak with ghosts. They also contact the spirit world using spirit boards or Ouija boards. These flat boards decorated with letters, numbers, and other symbols are supposedly used by spirits to communicate with the living.

Today there are countless psychic mediums or spirit messengers throughout the world. In the United States mediums perform readings for clients at carnivals, street fairs, and in storefronts. And anyone who types "spiritual medium" into an Internet search engine will find over 200,000 listings for mediums, most of whom claim to consult with the dead for paying clients.

Skeptics say most efforts to communicate with the dead are not based on reality, since there is no scientific proof of life after death. Lost love and a need to have answers to unanswered questions are two of the reasons people try to communicate with those in the spirit world. And many who do try to reach out to dead friends or relatives are in a vulnerable state and willing to believe the unbelievable when working with mediums according to Robert T. Carroll, author of The Skeptic's Dictionary Web site:

> [People participating in] readings must co-operate. Fortunately for the medium, most . . . [are] eager for the reader to succeed and are willing to work hard to find personal meaning in whatever the reader throws out. In a successful . . . reading, the [client] will be convinced that the accuracy of the reading was not due to her ability and willingness to cooperate but rather to the powers of . . . mediumship.[3]

Yet 32 percent of Americans surveyed by the Gallup organization said they believe the spirits of dead people can come back to earth and communicate with the living. It is common for spouses to speak with dead husbands or wives, parents to talk with deceased children, and children to communicate with departed parents. Spiritualism researcher Bob Olson states why this is so:

> While spiritual insight about life after death will not eliminate your grief, it can change your grieving experience from one of hopelessness, distress and fear to one of hope, comfort and peace. It is the difference

Did You Know?
According to a 2005 poll, more than two-thirds, or 68 percent, of people in Great Britain believe in the existence of ghosts and spirits.

Communicating with the Dead

According to a 2005 Gallup poll, 3 in 4 Americans admit to having at least one paranormal belief.

Of Those Believing in Paranormal Activity, Percent Believing That . . .

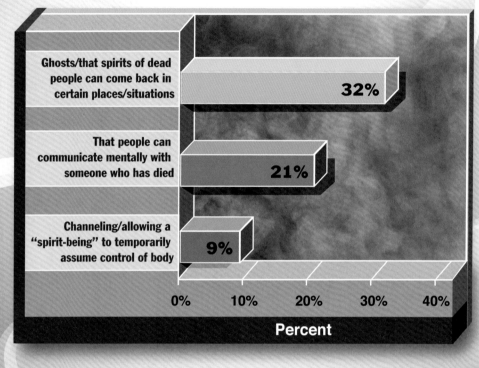

Ghosts/that spirits of dead people can come back in certain places/situations — **32%**

That people can communicate mentally with someone who has died — **21%**

Channeling/allowing a "spirit-being" to temporarily assume control of body — **9%**

Percent: 0% 10% 20% 30% 40%

Source: David W. Moore and Gallup News Service, "Three in Four Americans Believe in Paranormal," June 16, 2005.

between wondering where your deceased loved one has gone, feeling a loss of connection with them and worrying if they are still suffering—OR . . . understanding that they are watching over you and can hear you speak to them, and believing that they are not suffering, but rather, celebrating their *homecoming* with those who had crossed over [died] before them.[4]

CHAPTER 1

A Medium in the Middle

Rita Berkowitz sees dead people. She also talks to them and makes drawings of their faces. As an ordained minister of the First Spiritualist Church of Quincy, Massachusetts, Berkowitz says she is a certified medium who "can see and communicate with those on the higher side of life [dead people]."[5] She says she has the ability to channel, or act as a pathway, for messages delivered by the spirits of departed loved ones who purportedly hover around her clients.

Berkowitz is one among thousands of mediums, or intermediaries, who interact between the living and the dead. Mediums are spirit messengers who allow humans to interact with ghosts, angels, or spirits of the dead. Communications from the other world may consist of rapping or loud noises, spoken or written words, pictures, or garbled sounds that are difficult to understand. In recent decades some mediums have become well known for their exploits. Mediums such as Sylvia Browne, John Edward, George Anderson, and James van Praagh are best-selling authors who sell millions of books. These channelers of the dead also have their own TV shows and have appeared on *20/20*, *60 Minutes*, *Larry King Live*, and *Oprah*.

A Rapping Spirit

The widespread popularity of mediums in the digital age can be traced back to 1848, when two sisters innocently started the spiritualism craze. The girls, Kate and Maggie Fox, were not trained mediums or religious thinkers. But millions of people came to believe that the Fox sisters had supernatural talents that allowed them to communicate with the dead.

The sisters lived with their parents, John and Margaret Fox, in Arcadia, New York, a small town near Rochester. The family had just moved into their new house when the girls noticed some very strange occurrences. They described hearing knocking sounds within the walls and seeing furniture move around the rooms.

On one occasion, 11-year-old Maggie imitated the knocking sound by snapping her fingers. What followed seemed to defy explanation. Maggie snapped 5 times, and the spirit responded with 5 knocks. After several more tries, 14-year-old Kate began clapping, and the sounds she made were repeated within the walls. When asked to rap out the children's ages, the spirit did so, knocking 11 times for Maggie and 14 for Kate.

The Fox sisters promptly developed a code for the phantom to respond to questions, rapping twice for yes or not rapping at all when the answer was no. When asked if it was a human being, there was silence. When asked if it was a spirit, two loud raps were made.

The Dead Peddler

John Fox invited his neighbors in to watch the bizarre events. Several hundred people crowded into the small home and milled around in the yard, peering in windows. They watched in stunned amazement as the Fox sisters purportedly coaxed the entity to reveal more information. Using a code to represent letters of the alphabet, the spirit revealed that its name was Charles B. Rosna, a peddler who was murdered in 1843 and buried in the cellar. Upon hearing this news, several men descended excitedly to the basement and began digging. They were able to find a few small pieces of bone that might have been human or animal. Although most of the neighbors were taken in by the ghostly performance, several skeptics searched the house thoroughly. They were looking for loose boards, flapping shingles, hidden assistants, or other rational sources for the sounds.

The unusual events in Arcadia continued for days and soon attracted the attention of reporter E.E. Lewis. In late May 1848 Lewis described the events in a pamphlet called *A Report of the Mysterious Noises Heard in the House of John D. Fox, in Hydesville, Arcadia, Wayne County*. Before long the pamphlet about the Fox sisters was reprinted in big city newspapers along the East Coast. Hundreds more people flocked to Arcadia to hear the spirit talk. By this time John and Margaret Fox had become concerned about all the attention being showered on their girls. They decided to send them to the home of family friends Amy and Isaac Post—at least for a while. Rather than calming the situation, the Posts made matters worse. They were convinced that the Fox girls were mediums and spread the word about their talents.

OPPOSITE: Kate and Maggie Fox, shown in this portrait with their older sister Leah, convinced millions that they could communicate with the spirit world. The sisters developed a code that supposedly allowed spirits to respond to their questions.

Circles of Investigation

By 1850 Kate and Maggie were joined by an older sister, Leah, and together they held large public gatherings. People would ask the sisters questions, and the girls would respond with mysterious replies said to come from the spirit world. Each event might be attended by up to 100 "investigators," as people interested in spiritualism were called. The gatherings were called "circles of investigation." Today they are known as séances.

In this era before electric lights, movies, and TV, séances became a popular form of home entertainment. Across the United States, mediums organized gatherings around dining room tables where families came to speak to the spirits of the departed. If séance members, or sitters, were fortunate, an apparition might put on a show. Sitters reported that séance tables tipped, loud crashes shook walls, piano keys tinkled, and odd smells and smoke wafted through rooms. Sometimes an actual ghost would manifest out of thin air. In *Talking to the Dead*, author Barbara Weisberg describes some of the unusual events reported at a Fox séance in 1850: "[The] room sprang to life, as in a haunted house nightmare; a window curtain rolled up and down, a lounge shook violently, bureau drawers slammed open and shut, and a common spinning wheel seemed to be in motion, making a very natural buzz of the spindle."[6]

Led by the Fox sisters, the spiritualism fad continued to grow in cities across the United States. In 1854 the New York City Circle had hundreds of members and held public meetings and lectures on Broadway, the city's busiest street. In Providence, Rhode Island, there were 50 mediums at work. And after the Fox sisters visited Cincinnati, it was reported that 1,200 mediums set up shop there.

Not everyone was convinced that mediums were ac-

Did You Know?

James van Praagh was the first medium to perform spirit readings on American TV with his 1995 NBC show, *The Other Side.*

tually communicating with the dead. Renowned author Charles Dickens attended an 1860 séance in London held by a woman called Mrs. Marshall. He observed movements of a table and heard the sounds of a guitar played by invisible hands and a bell ringing in the dark. However, Dickens wrote that it was "due to trickery, the only 'mediums' in the case being Mrs. Marshall's fingers and toes"[7] creating the noises said to be messages from spirits.

"Many Moons Ago I Lived"

Marshall was taking advantage of the belief that some people, called physical mediums, can cause ghosts to materialize; that is, create some sort of actual presence in the material world. Spirits that are materialized by physical mediums may tip tables, shake furniture, play instruments, or rattle the curtains. Communication is often achieved through an object called a planchette. This is a heart-shaped piece of wood with little legs that either moves a pencil over paper or is used to spell out words on a Ouija board. Its movement is guided by hands of the medium and sitters, which they place lightly on the planchette during a séance.

One of the most famous cases of purported spirit communications with a planchette occurred in 1913 when a St. Louis housewife, Pearl Curran, was using a Ouija board one day with her mother and several friends. Curran thought Ouija boards were silly children's toys, but to her surprise, the planchette began spelling out a cryptic message: "Many moons ago I lived. Again I come. Patience Worth is my name."[8]

Over the course of the next several hours, the ghost of Patience Worth spelled out an amazing story on the Ouija board. Using old-fashioned words such as "thee" and

Did You Know?

After the terrorist strike on the World Trade Center on September 11, 2001, medium John Edward planned to contact the spirits of those who died in the attack, but that episode of his television show was canceled due to widespread public outrage.

"thou," the spirit said it was the ghost of a farmwoman from Dorsetshire, England. She moved to America in the late 1600s and was killed in an Indian attack.

Although there were other sitters when Patience Worth appeared, it soon became clear that the ghost was communicating through Curran. Fascinated, Curran began spending all her time at the Ouija board while a friend wrote down the messages that came to her through the planchette. However, the communications from Worth began coming so fast that it was impossible to translate them through the Ouija board. It was then that Curran discovered that Worth's messages were forming in her mind and she did not need the board. Instead Curran entered a trance and began reciting the communications to sitters. Soon she learned to record the messages herself using a pen and paper or a typewriter.

Although Curran only had an eighth-grade education, she became a prolific author of books allegedly communicated to her by Patience Worth. For the next 7 years, Curran channeled 400,000 words that filled 29 volumes. The books consisted of 2,500 poems, 6 full-length historical novels, plus plays, short stories, and other writings, including a 1,200-page epic, *The Sorry Tale*, about the life of Jesus. The books enjoyed widespread popularity, and hundreds of people came to visit Curran to watch her work.

Trance Mediums

Once Curran stopped using the Ouija board and began communicating while in a hypnotic, dreamlike state, she became what is known as a trance medium. In this condition the ghost purportedly takes over the medium's body and sends messages to the mind or manipulates the hand to write missives. On the American Hauntings Web site, researcher Troy Taylor explains Curran's methods:

A decades-old photograph appears to show participants in a séance holding hands and concentrating as spirits seem to cause a table to float while the medium's arms and legs are tied to a chair. During the early 1900s, séance participants reported many strange occurrences, including loud crashes, odd smells, and shaking furniture.

Pearl explained that . . . images would appear to her. She would see the details of each scene. If two characters were talking along a road, she would see the roadway, the grass on either side of it and perhaps the landscape in the distance. If they spoke a foreign language, she would hear them speaking but above them, she would hear the voice of Patience as she interpreted the speech and indicated what part of the dialogue she wanted in the story. She would sometimes even see herself in the scenes, standing as an onlooker or moving between the characters.[9]

Curran's books have been analyzed by scholars, who found the details historically accurate. The plots were well-constructed, and some of the stories were written in an authentic Old English vocabulary that Curran had no way of knowing. Those who challenge the concept of trance mediumship say that while Curran's output was highly unusual, she must have been writing from her subconscious. Whatever the case, after seven years, Curran claimed that Worth stopped talking to her, and her communications came to an end.

Automatic Speech

When Curran first became a trance medium, she used what was called "automatic speech" to dictate communications from Patience Worth. Automatic speech is based on the idea that a spirit can use a medium as a channel for communicating with the living. To do so, the medium enters a trance and uses his or her mouth to speak for the spirit. One of the most celebrated cases of automatic speech involves Jane Roberts.

In December 1963 the 34-year-old Roberts was holding a séance with her husband, Robert Butts, in their apartment in Elmira, New York. Roberts began receiving messages from a spirit who called himself Seth. This being was so powerful that Roberts started to conduct twice-

Cold-Reading Techniques

The So, You Wanna Be a Psychic? Web site explores facts used by cold readers to ferret out information during spirit readings:

The causes and speed of a death can be zeroed in pretty quickly: cancer, chest, head, sudden or abrupt. . . .

A family member is usually a grandparent, parent, sibling or child. . . . A person sought will most of the time be a fond memory. Important objects are usually books, letters, jewelry, or similar gifts. Hair [of the deceased] can be brown, black, blonde, red. . . .

Of course, the most used bait for [mediums] is letters of the alphabet. There are 26 letters in the alphabet, but the letters t, s, c, m, f, p (and vowels) are at the beginning of approximately three-quarters of all words. Furthermore, while there are 3.2 million first names, one-third of the population has one of only 300 of them. . . . Given the number of significant people in our lives, it is not surprising that tricks can be found to maximize probabilities. Even then, lots of misses can occur.

Alleee and Franc, "So, You Wanna Be a Psychic?" Insolitology. www.insolitology.com.

weekly sessions with him. Her husband wrote down his messages in shorthand. By January 1970 Roberts had conducted 511 sessions with what she called the discarnate (lacking a physical body) Seth entity. The messages from the sessions were gathered into a 300-page book called *The Seth Material*.

Subjects covered by Seth include the nature of reality, time, physical matter, and the meaning of God. Seth also talked about life after death, the secrets of success, causes of illnesses, and how people could develop their inner senses to live better lives.

The Seth Material became a best seller. Although the book is often dense and difficult to follow, it is credited for laying the foundation of the New Age movement. New Age believers engage in practices such as channeling, astrology, out-of-body experiences, crystal healing, fortune-telling, and meditation. These subjects were discussed in detail by Seth, and many are used to communicate with the dead.

Clear Seeing

Another type of medium is called a mental medium or oracle. These people use clairvoyance, or "clear seeing," to visualize ghosts in the mind even when the spirits are not physically present. While seeing the ghost in the "mind's eye," mental mediums communicate with the apparitions. Some mediums can do this in a normal, awake state, while others use crystal balls or some other aid to help them gaze into the other world.

In 2006 a British clairvoyant, Lisa Williams, became a hit on American TV with her show, *Lisa Williams: Life Among the Dead*, on the Lifetime network. Williams is sometimes called a "punk clairvoyant" because of her spiky hair and the fact that she was once a lead singer in an alternative rock band. But Williams says her link to the supernatural world is through her grandmother, the world-renowned psychic Frances Glazebrook, who was a secret psychic adviser to the British royal family and several American corporate leaders.

On *Life Among the Dead*, Williams investigates haunted houses and conducts street interviews with strangers. When she channels the dead through clairvoyance, she often brings people to tears. One episode showed Williams telling a woman about her husband's death as a soldier in Iraq. In another show, she talked to a tour bus driver about his mother, who was watching over him from heaven. Williams also claims she has spoken to deceased movie stars such as Bob Hope, Natalie Wood, and Marilyn Monroe, along with musician Ray Charles and Britain's Princess Diana.

Critics believe Williams and other clairvoyants rely on earthly tricks called cold reading or "shotgunning." These techniques are used to convince clients that the mediums are channeling spirits. A cold reader makes general statements while trying to learn the name of a dead relative. An example is provided by skeptics known as Alleee and Franc on the So, You Wanna Be a Psychic? Web site: "Is there someone related to an M? I'm seeing a M-A-R name. Martha, Margaret. . . ."[10] If the name is correct, the client is amazed. If it is wrong, the medium quickly moves on to another common initial, such as S. Studies have shown that people forget the incorrect guesses of the cold reader and are astounded when the proper name is finally produced.

When guessing problems, the cold reader relies on basic facts. For example, heart disease is the number one killer of men. Therefore, a medium might say, "I see a heart problem with a father-figure in your family, a

Did You Know?

Skeptic James Randi offers a $1 million prize to anyone who can demonstrate supernatural or paranormal abilities under scientific testing conditions.

British clairvoyant Lisa Williams claims to have spoken with the spirits of many prominent people, including Princess Diana (pictured). Skeptics say Williams and other clairvoyants rely on techniques that have nothing to do with channeling spirits.

father, a grandfather, an uncle, a cousin. . . . I'm definitively seeing chest pain here for a father-figure in your family."[11]

Cold readers also can learn a lot about a client by analyzing his or her age. For example, if someone is over 30, they might be missing a parent. If a client is over 50, they might wish to communicate to a dead child or spouse. If a guess is wrong, the medium can quickly move on to another line of thought.

There are over 20 cold-reading techniques used by TV mediums and others in the business. They have been perfected over the years, but few believers are aware of them. And as long as people are desperate to communicate with dead relatives, there will be no shortage of mediums who will use tricks and, perhaps, real talents to communicate with those on the other side.

CHAPTER 2

Speaking with Spooks

Harry Price was a well known investigator of the paranormal; that is, unusual experiences that defy scientific explanation. In 1922 Price visited medium William Hope's London photography studio. Hope had gained fame and fortune providing his customers with what he called celestial photos. These pictures showed the person who was posing surrounded by hazy images said to be dead relatives, friends, and even pets.

Believers in celestial, or spirit, photography said that such photos provide proof of life after death. The pictures are described as a form of communication in which spirits are able to create images on film from beyond the grave using their supernatural thought patterns. However, Price was not convinced of Hope's talents.

After posing for the medium-photographer, Price discovered that Hope was using darkroom tricks to make spirit photographs. The photographer used images from old photographic negatives and superimposed them over the pictures of the sitters. Price created an uproar among British spiritualists when he exposed Hope as a fraud in a report published in the *Journal of the Society for Psychical Research*.

Despite his reputation as a tough paranormal investigator, Price believed in ghosts. In fact, he spent most of his life investigating haunted houses and attempting to communicate with the dead. But unlike most mediums, Price used scientific methods to hunt ghosts. Although he viewed most claims made by mediums with skepticism, he maintained a belief that it was possible to communicate with those on the other side.

"Inquire If It Is a Spirit"

Mediums rely on trances, Ouija boards, crystal balls, and automatic writing. But the tools of paranormal investigators, which are still in use today, tend to be more mundane. Investigators might sprinkle baking flour on the floor of a haunted house to detect phantom footprints. Chalk is used to draw rings around furniture legs and objects on tables to determine if they have been moved by ghosts. Highly accurate thermometers are used to detect slight temperature variations said to be caused by ghosts entering or leaving a room. And tools such as flashlights and candles are employed by investigators who spend most of their time waiting in the dark for apparitions to appear. Many paranormal investigators never see a ghost, but in *The Most Haunted House in England*, Price provides guidelines for communication when ghosts materialize: "[Do] not approach, but ascertain name, age, sex, origin, cause of visit, if in trouble, and possible alleviation. Inquire if it is a spirit. Ask figure to return, suggesting exact time and place. Do not move until the figure disappears. Note exact method of vanishing."[12]

Messages on the Walls

One of Price's most extensive investigations took place at the Borley Rectory, a sprawling Victorian home located near the small town of Borley in rural Essex. The rectory, or home where the parish priest lived, was constructed in 1863 on the site of the twelfth-century Borley Church. A fourteenth-century

monastery also once stood on the grounds.

Borley Rectory was allegedly haunted for years. But when Price began his investigation in 1929, the home's occupants, the Reverend G.E. Smith and his wife, reported hearing odd noises such as phantom footsteps dragging across the floor and a woman's voice shrieking. Smith also reported seeing strange lights in the windows, along with a headless coachman driving a phantom coach. The ghostly events were seemingly harmless, but the Smiths moved out as Price was beginning his investigation.

When the new residents, the Reverend Lionel Foyster and his wife, Marianne, moved into the rectory in 1930, the ghostly activities increased dramatically. On some nights, while the couple cringed under their bedsheets, windows shattered, furniture was loudly dragged from room to room, and piercing knocks echoed through the

In the 1920s, residents of Borley Rectory (pictured here after a fire) reported hearing mysterious sounds, including dragging footsteps and a shrieking voice. They also reported strange sights such as unexplained lights and a headless coachman driving a phantom carriage.

house. The apparition seemed to take particular delight in tormenting Marianne. As Troy Taylor writes in "Borley Rectory: The History of 'The Most Haunted House in England'":

> [Marianne Foyster] was thrown from her bed at night, slapped by invisible hands, forced to dodge heavy objects which flew at her day and night, and was once almost suffocated with a mattress. Soon after, there began to appear a series of scrawled messages on the walls of the house, written by an unknown hand. They seemed to be pleading with Mrs. Foyster, using phrases like "Marianne, please help" . . . and "Marianne light mass prayers."[13]

Price was particularly interested in these spirit communications because he had never seen such writings in his years as a paranormal investigator.

The Murdered Nun

The violent events surrounding Marianne Foyster were typical of poltergeist activity. Poltergeists, German for "noisy spirits," are not like ghosts because they commit a wide range of bizarre pranks, including breaking objects, provoking spontaneous fires and floods, whipping up strong winds on a calm day, and even placing excrement on walls. People have claimed that they were pinched, bitten, hit, or sexually assaulted by poltergeists. And according to investigator Raymond Bayless in *The Enigma of the Poltergeist*, spirits can also communicate with yells, "screams, bellows, whistlings, whispers, laughs, sobs, grunts, and every imaginable sound possible."[14]

In the case of Borley Rectory, the poltergeist activity was so horrible that the Foytsers were driven from the building, leaving it to sit abandoned for several years. Price finally rented the rectory in 1937 and began a year-long, round-the-clock investigation. Accompanied by several paranormal investigators and a journalist from the British Broadcasting Corporation, Price verified hundreds of ghostly events occurring in the rectory.

There was a constant barrage of odd noises, including clicks, thumps, taps, footsteps, and crashes that sounded like dishes falling in the kitchen. Puddles of brown water and glue-like substances appeared and disappeared suddenly, and foul odors similar to a backed-up toilet sickened several ghost hunters.

With no obvious solution to the mysterious haunting presenting itself, Price became determined to contact the spirits. Although he had exposed fraud perpetrated by a dozen mediums during séances, Price decided to hold his own spirit circle. He recruited three other ghost hunters to gather around a table in the parlor of the rectory. The men rested their hands lightly on a planchette over a piece of paper. After several nights of silence, contact was finally made with a spirit named Marie Lairre. By posing a series of yes-or-no questions, Price was able to understand the story of her death in the seventeenth century.

Lairre said that she was a French nun who left her convent to marry Henry Waldegrave, a member of a wealthy family whose manor home once stood on the site of the rectory. The marriage was short and unhappy. During one of their arguments, Waldegrave strangled Lairre and buried her remains in the cellar. Lairre told the assembled investigators that she continued to haunt the rectory because she wanted her bones to be exhumed and moved to a cemetery so they could be buried with a requiem

Marianne

I CANNOT UNDERSTAN

TELL ME MORE

Marianne,

I STILL CANNOT UNDERSTAND

PLEASE. TELL ME MORE,

mass conducted by a Catholic priest.

Price searched the rectory basement for bones, but none were recovered. The rectory burned to the ground several years later, and Price did not return until 1943, when he found several fragile human bones under the brick floor in the cellar where the house once stood. He gave the remains a proper burial, and no further paranormal activities were reported at the ruins of the rectory.

Grunts and Groans

The poltergeist of Marie Lairre purportedly communicated a coherent message concerning her wish for a proper burial. However, it is extremely unusual for the noisy spirits to explain their desires to investigators clearly. More often, they seem to communicate through a single word, a threatening sentence, a song, or endless paragraphs filled with bizarre lectures.

The words might be in an unknown language or simply in gibberish. And the communications can materialize out of thin air or be projected from a range of items, including vases, flowers, or trumpets. Whatever the case, poltergeist expressions seem to develop and change during the course of a haunting, according to Colin Wilson in *Poltergeist! A Study in Destructive Haunting*:

> Poltergeist voices . . . do not sound like ordinary human voices; at least not to begin with. It seems as if the entity is having to master a strange medium, to form sounds into words. . . . Most talking . . . poltergeists begin in a guttural voice that sounds as if it is made up from grunts and groans; [in one case the spirit] made gasping, whispering noises more like an asthmatic cough. Gradually the voice developed until it was a low audible whisper. . . . [The voice] graduated from a whisper to a normal voice. . . . Then it began to use bad language—again a common characteristic of talking [poltergeists].[15]

"Evil Spirits Go Away"

One of the oddest cases of poltergeist communications comes from paranormal investigator Hans Holzer, who has written 138 books on the supernatural and occult. The events began in a haunted home on Elizabeth Street in Tyler, Texas, in 1964. The house was inhabited by Howard Beaird; his wife, Johnnie; and their son, Andy.

At first the family suffered through typical poltergeist experiences. As Beaird told Holzer:

> Andy and I would go to bed, and as soon as we turned out the light we were plagued by hordes of June bugs of all sizes, which would hit us on our heads and faces, some glancing off on the floor, others landing on the bed, and some missing us entirely and smashing themselves against the metal window blinds. Night after night we fought these bugs in the dark, grabbing those that landed on the bed and throwing them against the blinds as hard as we could.[16]

The Beairds were also troubled with fires. On one occasion, Howard smelled smoke and rushed into the bathroom to find the wall heater on high, burning paper towels that someone—or something—had stuffed into the burners. Howard began to suspect his wife, Johnnie, was mentally ill and starting the fires. He sent her to live with her sister-in-law in Daingerfield, Texas, about 100 miles (161km) from Tyler.

Johnnie's absence did not solve the problems. In fact, after she left, the poltergeist began communicating with Howard and Andy. While lying in bed one night, Howard heard a disembodied voice. Although it did not sound like Johnnie, it began telling stories from the early years of their marriage that only she would know. In the weeks that followed, at least six other voices seemed to be haunting the house, emerging out of thin air and carrying on conversations with Howard. The voices included family acquaintances, those of people who had been dead for years, and one friend who died in a car accident

Was Harry Price a Fraud?

Harry Price impressed many skilled paranormal researchers in his day, but some have come to believe he was a fraud. In the 2006 article "Ghostbuster or Fraud" from London's *Daily Express*, Simon Edge explains:

> Within hours of Price's arrival at [Borley] rectory, a string of new phenomena—bangs, clattering, keys being thrown and coins raining down—were observed. The rector's wife later said: "We could not help being led to suppose that Mr. Price was producing some of the effects."
>
> When windows mysteriously smashed themselves as he showed a journalist round, the latter noted that Price kept taking a step back just before it happened, and there was a swishing sound as if a [rock] had been thrown. . . . [The] journalist recalled: "I got hold of him and found two of his coat-pockets full of stones. He stammered but offered no excuses or explanations. . . . The journalist said he would expose Price but . . . his newspaper's lawyers feared the ghostbuster might sue and the story was dropped.

Simon Edge, "Ghostbuster or Fraud," The Harry Price Web site. www.harryprice.co.uk.

only days after his voice was heard.

Meanwhile the bug raids continued, and other dangerous objects, such as carpenter nails and large chunks of rock salt, were seen flying around the house. The poltergeist also made piles of filth appear in Johnnie's bed. These consisted of mud mixed with broken pieces of soap, old hair, and burned matches. The first time this happened, the mess was accompanied by a note written in a young child's scrawl that said, "Evil spirits go away."[17]

This note signaled the beginning of a long-running correspondence between the spirit world and the Beairds as notes and letters began to appear out of thin air on a regular basis. Many were in Johnnie's handwriting, although she resided in a distant town. The notes seemed to predict the future. Names of friends and relatives were written next to the dates they would allegedly die, ranging from several years in the future to the year 2018. Another note said "Johnnie Beaird—Death 1991."[18]

Mrs. Elliot and Mr. Gree

By December 1965 Howard and Andy were being bombarded with 10 to 15 notes every day. Many materialized out of thin air, folded themselves before the eyes of the amazed Beairds, and either hit them or fell to the floor. Some were written by people they knew, living and dead, and others were from unknown people or public figures such as Marilyn Monroe, who died in 1962. The handwriting, however, often seemed to be a disjointed style similar to Johnnie's or Andy's. Several of the ghostly writers made repeat visits, such as a Mrs. Elliot, a friend who had been dead for several years, and a Mr. Gree, who was unknown to the family. The notes, while discussing other spirits, family members, and the events that were taking place in the Beaird household, were conversational in tone and read like personal letters that close friends might write. For example, Mrs. Elliot often worried about Andy and imagined conflicts between the teenager and his parents. Discussing these matters in a disjointed note, Mrs.

Elliot wrote a rather disturbing missive about taking Andy into the spirit world, where she could care for him:

> Howard, I need to write you notes. Junior has had to worry so much. Why do you mind him coming with me? He would be happy. . . . In the meantime I will help John [Johnnie] and him. He could play music and he would be great at seventeen. He would also like to take care of the house. John would get so much better. You would be better financially and Junior could get better. . . . You had better pay attention because he wants to come. I have all the divine right to take him.[19]

Mrs. Elliot and Mr. Gree also communicated with disembodied voices that could be heard throughout the house. On one occasion, Mr. Gree used the kitchen telephone, moving the rotary dial with invisible fingers and speaking into the mouthpiece as it hovered in the air. The conversation was apparently private as the spirit asked Howard and Andy to leave the room while it was talking.

Finally, in April 1968 Howard and Andy Beaird left their house of horrors on Elizabeth Street, never to return. After the move, they were rejoined by Johnnie and the family was not bothered by any further incidents involving poltergeists.

There is little research available to explain the bizarre communications experienced by the Beairds. Unlike the story of Borley Rectory, there is no satisfying ending in which the spirit communicates a problem that needs to be solved. But Holzer determined that both

Andy and Johnnie were mentally unstable individuals. After conducting a detailed analysis of the handwritten notes, Holzer concluded that they were written by either Andy or Johnnie, whose hands were controlled by spirits of the dead. As Holzer writes, "Actual non-physical entities were, in fact, using the untapped energies of these two unfortunate individuals to express themselves in the physical world."[20]

This ghostly energy, according to believers, can dematerialize objects and rematerialize them in different places. This would explain the notes falling out of the air. Because the unidentified poltergeists occupied the house itself, the activity ceased when the family moved. The people who later moved into the Elizabeth Street house also noticed odd noises and occasional movements of furniture but purportedly did not have mentally unstable family members to draw poltergeists out of the spirit world.

Paranormal State

Mysterious tales from paranormal investigators have long fascinated the public. Perhaps this explains the popularity of the reality show *Paranormal State* on A&E. In 2009 the show followed the real-life activities of student investigators in the Pennsylvania State University Paranormal Research Society (PRS). Although no spooks have spoken on camera, the show demonstrates typical activities of ghost hunters as they search for spirits. And since the show first aired to 2.5 million viewers in December 2007, the PRS has been inundated with thousands of requests by frightened people who believe their homes are haunted. While most investigations would probably lead to dead ends, a few might uncover spirits who are dying to deliver messages from beyond the grave.

CHAPTER 3

Spirit Guides

The belief in spirits is universal, shared by nearly every religion and culture. In Western culture the spirit is sometimes called the soul. And the soul is said to be immortal—it lives forever. Some believe that after death the soul resides in heaven or on "a higher plane" with a creator. Others think that souls called spirit guides can return to earth for a variety of purposes. These bodiless beings provide aid, comfort, friendship, and physical healing. As psychic, author, and TV personality Sylvia Browne explains in *The Other Side and Back*:

> The Spirit Guide's job is to urge, nudge, encourage, advise, support, and, as their title suggests, guide us on our life's path. . . . Their vantage point on the Other Side gives them direct access to God's divine knowledge, and they also enjoy every spirit's enviable ability to be in several places at once, unencumbered by these bodies we make such a big deal out of having.[21]

Connection with the Divine Intelligence

Dozens of best-selling authors, including Browne, have written books about spirit guides in recent years. But the belief in such beings goes back much further. It is part of a long tradition in Native American teachings that spirits of deceased ancestors walk among the living.

Many Native Americans perform rituals and ceremonies to strengthen the connection between the spirit world and the earthly plane of existence. These rites include singing, dancing, and playing music, which help participants attain a trancelike state in which they can communicate with spirit guides. As the Native American Drumming Circle Web site explains:

> One of the most beautiful indigenous customs is the love and . . . power of sound, drumming and dancing to create a direct connection with the Great Spirit. . . . We begin by playing drums, flutes, and any other native instruments. We build the energy to a point where . . . our Spirit guides . . . can be felt in a more personal, individual and unique way. . . . Through this connection with the Divine Intelligence and Wisdom of the Universe, we connect and uplift our spirit.[22]

"He Will Give You a Blessing"

With their deep connection to spirit guides, Native American beliefs have been adopted by white Americans and Europeans over the years. In the nineteenth and early twentieth centuries, many prominent American spiritualists claimed that their spirit guides were Native Americans with names such as White Hawk and Running Bear. This phenomenon was not confined to white spiritualists, however. An African American medium named Leafy Anderson claimed to be guided by the spirit of Black Hawk, a Fox Indian leader, warrior, and healer who died in 1838. Anderson founded the African American Spiritual Church

Did You Know?

The renowned nineteenth-century medium Madame Blavatsky claimed to be advised by spirit guides from India and Tibet.

A Cheyenne dance group and a Zuni Drumming Circle perform ceremonial dances and music. Some Native Americans use drumming, dancing, and singing to connect with spirit guides.

movement in New Orleans in the 1920s. The church, still in existence today, features rituals, hymns, and ceremonies honoring Black Hawk's spirit. Anderson's niece, Edmonia Caldwell, is a bishop in the church. She describes Black Hawk's powers of healing and justice: "[Leafy Anderson] healed through Black Hawk. I have healed through Black Hawk. . . . But you have to use him right. You can't ask him to harm. He'll help you, as a guide and [for] protection. People going to jail, he'll help you. But I've never known him to do dirty work. Only good things come to me [through him]. He will give you a blessing."[23]

Native American spirit guides are also familiar at the Cassadaga Spiritualist Camp, one of the oldest spiritualism communities in the United States. The Cassadaga

Spiritualist Camp, near Orlando, Florida, was founded in 1894 by New Yorker George Colby, who said he was led to central Florida by a Native American spirit guide called Seneca. Today 25 mediums permanently reside in the community, which is referred to as a camp. The mediums conduct séances, channel spirits, and provide healing and counseling through the use of spirit guides. For example, according to *Cassadaga: The South's Oldest Spiritualist Community*, medium Jim Watson has a spirit guide that is "a seven-foot Native American named White Bear who was revealed to him during his training as a medium. For Watson, White Bear has become a continuous presence that he talks to as he would any good friend."[24]

Psychic Sylvia Browne also relies on an indigenous American spirit guide, named Iena. Browne says Iena is an Aztec Incan woman born in Colombia in 1500. She was killed by Spanish conquistadors, or conquerors, in 1520.

While many people are interested in Native American religions and claim to have Indian spirit guides, not everyone appreciates this trend. Cherokee author Orrin Lewis, cocreator of a Web site on Native American languages, history, culture, and beliefs, comments: "Hucksters [are] pretending to be Native American shamans to scam money off of people. . . . [I] suggest ignoring and avoiding information about American Indian [spirit guides] presented by anyone . . . [claiming] to be American Indian shamans, talking about . . . New Age things."[25]

Listening to the Band

Many types of spirit guides are said to provide wisdom. During the second half of the nineteenth century, mediums frequently called upon the spirits of America's founders. As Barbara Weisberg writes: "Benjamin Franklin

Street signs clearly mark an intersection in the Florida community known as Cassadaga Spiritualist Camp. The mediums who live in the community channel spirits, conduct séances, and provide healing and counseling with help from spirit guides.

probably visited more often than any other famous spirit. Given the multiple identities he had assumed during his lifetime—inventor, trickster, magician, founding father, and diplomat—he was an ideal representative from the other world."[26]

Even today, dead politicians, scientists, and celebrities are regularly called upon to act as spirit guides. Psychic Willow Sibert claims to take advice from what she calls a band of famous spirit guides. Her Web site contains a message from them:

> We are a collective energy of many souls and former personalities that have existed on the earth plane in physical form throughout the ages. Our personalities

include Albert Einstein, Benjamin Franklin, Marie Curie, Thomas Jefferson, Amelia Earhart . . . Thomas Edison, Isaac Newton . . . and many others. We speak as one, and we speak as individuals. . . .

Just like the band, or an orchestra, the music is sweet; the message is powerful.[27]

Sights, Smells, and Spider Webs

For most people, spirit guides do not appear as celebrities but as friends, relatives, or even total strangers. Unlike ghosts, whose appearance is often unwanted, spirit guides generally make their presence known only to those who are seeking them. But the spirits do not often arrive as visible beings. Instead the cosmic entities may announce their presence through sight, smell, or other senses.

Some see their guides as floating or flickering lights, appearing out of the corner of the eye. Others know their spirit guide has arrived when they perceive certain

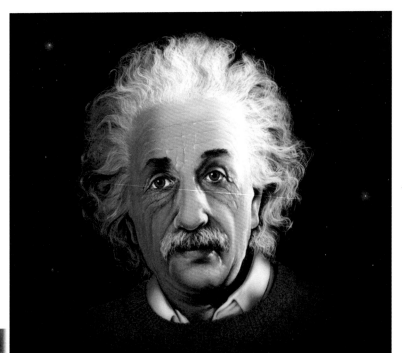

Spirit guides are said to offer wisdom to those who communicate with them. Psychic Willow Sibert claims the renowned physicist Albert Einstein is one of her spirit guides.

smells. For example, some recognize the arrival of an aunt spirit by the aroma of her perfume or the presence of an uncle spirit by the odor of his cigar.

People may also feel spirit guides in various ways. Often it is reported that the temperature suddenly moves up or down when a spirit is present. Those who perceive spirits, called percipients, might also get the creepy feeling of having walked into a spider web. As Rita S. Berkowitz and Deborah S. Romaine explain, "Sometimes a spirit attempts to 'reach out and touch'—which, of course, isn't especially practical for an intangible, discarnate [bodiless] entity! You might feel the energy of the spirit's presence [like a spider web] making contact with your skin."[28]

Because they lack physical form, it is said that spirit guides most easily appear in dreams. Those who wish to remember the advice of dream spirits are advised to keep a journal next to the bed to write down the messages. In *Spirit Allies*, Christopher Penczak provides a method for contacting spirit guides in dreams. Before going to bed, invoke your spirit allies by saying, "I call upon my spirit [guides] . . . who come for my highest good, in perfect love and trust."[29]

Dream messages are often difficult to understand. But sometimes the communications obviously contain important information that should not be ignored. As Berkowitz and Romaine write:

> Some of the most common and dramatic messages relate to health issues. A departed loved one might appear in a dream to tell you to schedule an appointment to have the doctor check out that mole on your neck. You do, and it turns to be skin cancer, caught in the earliest stages so it ends up

Did You Know?
After George Chapman performed spiritual surgery on Joe Bernard Hutton in 1966, the patient noticed a long mark, about 5 inches (12.7cm) long, that looked exactly like a surgical incision.

being nothing but a minor inconvenience. Ignoring these messages causes the dreams to become more persistent and perhaps more graphic or startling, until finally you "get" it and see the doctor.[30]

Diagnosing Disease

Whether or not they appear in dreams, spirit guides are often associated with healing the mind and body. They are said to provide guidance in two ways. Spirit guides are said to provide positive healing energy that directly aids those suffering from mental or physical problems. The spirits may also take a diagnostic approach, identifying medical problems.

Diagnostic spirit aid can be delivered by professional mediums. When clients with health issues visit Sylvia Browne, she relies on Iena to detect the trouble. Browne claims to have discovered that a woman who thought she was facing death from a rare blood disease was only suffering from an easily curable thyroid condition. She also advised a girl who was suffering from acute acne that she was allergic to dairy products. The girl stopped drinking milk and eating cheese, and her acne cleared up for the first time in years.

Browne says she can diagnose people through the telephone or even by letters sent through the mail. But she warns people that they should seek proper medical care and not rely on psychics or mediums to solve their health problems. However, she takes great pride in her ability to diagnose sickness, writing, "Throughout these many years, and after thousands of letters from clients and doctors reporting successful outcomes to my medical suggestions, the subject of health has become a source of profound satisfaction for me."[31]

Healing the Spirit

Browne receives advice from her Native American spirit guide, and this is the advice she passes along to clients. But some spiritual healers say they do not just receive advice from healers of the past. They say these healers actually communicate through them, using their bodies to heal the sick with spiritual energy. Those who make this claim are often trance mediums, who enter into a hypnotic state. In this condition spirit guides move their hands over a patient. But instead of performing physical operations with surgical tools, spiritual healers say they are healing what is called the aura of their patients. British-born spiritual healer and best-selling author Rosemary Altea explains the concept of the aura in *Proud Spirit*: "[Every] living thing has an aura. Our aura, or energy field, surrounds us, extending above and beyond the skin by several feet. . . . When we become physically sick, our ill health is mirrored in our aura, affects our aura, [and] often affects our spirit."[32]

Psychic Willow Sibert claims that pilot Amelia Earhart, who mysteriously disappeared during a 1937 flight, is one of several prominent people who act as her spirit guides.

Those who communicate with medical spirit guides believe that the aura is connected to the physical body. When a person's aura is healed, the body will also get well. This belief guided the 60-year career of George Chapman, who died in 2006 at age 85.

Chapman, who was a firefighter in Liverpool, England, lost his 4-month-old daughter in 1946. Distraught over her death, he conducted séances in hopes of contacting his daughter's spirit. At some point during these séances, he started channeling an entity calling himself Dr. Lang. When Dr. Lang communicated through Chapman, the Liverpool fireman abandoned his natural accent and spoke as a wealthy, educated London doctor. Mystified by the turn of events, Chapman searched through official records for doctors named Lang. He discovered that William Lang, who had died in 1937, had been a surgeon at London's Middlesex Hospital from 1880 to 1914. Fascinated, Chapman conducted a series of séances where he let Dr. Lang communicate through him. This purportedly led Chapman to discover many accurate facts about William Lang. Chapman describes his approach:

> [Dr. Lang] should be able to give dates, names and details of his earthly experiences that can be verified, and be able to discuss intimate matters with relatives and colleagues still on earth. . . . William Lang . . . satisfied all my demands. . . . Colleagues of Dr. Lang and the people whom he had treated . . . confirmed [I] was [channeling] the same Dr. Lang they had known.[33]

Dr. Lang instructed Chapman on methods spirits used to heal the auras of sick patients. By the early 1950s Chapman had become a globe-trotting healer who treated people in Britain, Switzerland, Germany, Spain, the United States, and elsewhere. By treating people's auras the spirit doctor was said to cure all manner of problems, including cataracts, arthritis, glaucoma, and even cancer.

Did You Know?

Brazilian spirit healer João de Deus, or "John of God," says several spirit doctors work through him and allow him to cure cancer, blindness, asthma, drug addiction, and other physical problems.

One of Chapman's most renowned cases concerned Joseph Tanguy, who was suffering from a deadly brain tumor in 1974. The young man had undergone an operation in a London hospital, but it was unsuccessful. He was told he had 6 months to live. Tanguy's doctor notified Chapman, who performed a spirit operation as Dr. Lang. After 2 healing sessions Dr. Lang notified Tanguy that he was cured. Within 5 months a medical examination revealed that the tumor had completely disappeared and the patient had fully recovered. The unnamed doctor who sent Tanguy to Chapman stated in writing: "I have . . . complete trust in sending to [Dr. Lang] those patients for whom all known therapies have failed. . . . The healing of Mr. Tanguy's brain tumor, which had been beyond all therapeutic resources, is a completely convincing example [of spirit healing]."[34]

When Chapman worked, the spirit of Dr. Lang worked through him and guided his hands. A description of the healer's methods came from a California lawyer named Morton B. Jackson, who suffered from a painful condition of the joints called rheumatoid spondylitis. When treating Jackson, Chapman took on the appearance of an old man with wrinkles and lines on his face. And he spoke as an elderly gentleman with the convincing bedside manner practiced by experienced surgeons. When Dr. Lang began his spirit operation, Jackson said he became

> aware of the sharp cracking noise of [Dr. Lang's] snapping fingers occasionally accompanied by instructions to Basil [Lang's son who died in 1928] and others apparently assisting him. The nature of the touch, while light, seemed consistent with the

Did You Know?
Healers called psychic surgeons channel spirit guides who allow them to reach into the bodies of patients and remove tumors, cancer cells, kidney stones, and other harmful material without surgical tools.

handling and utilization of invisible [surgical] instruments. . . . All this while . . . Dr. Lang explaining, as he went along, what it was he was doing and why.[35]

Skeptics have dismissed Dr. Lang as an act meant to fool patients into believing they are cured. But according to Chapman's obituary in the *London Telegraph*: "William Lang's daughter, Lyndon, and his granddaughter, Susan Fairtlough, confirmed not only that his speech and mannerisms were as they remembered them, but also that they discussed events and people who would have been unknown to George Chapman, who was not even in his teens when Lang retired from private medical practice."[36]

Working through Chapman's body, the spirit guide of Dr. Lang was said to have healed thousands of patients over the years. He performed healings on British celebrities such as actor Laurence Harvey and even cured medical problems in a surgeon and a dentist.

A Secondary Mission

The concept of channeling spirit guides to perform medical procedures is extremely controversial, and there is no scientific proof that spirit surgery is anything but an illusion. Therefore, the U.S. Federal Trade Commission has labeled spirit surgery as medical fraud and a "total hoax."[37] Despite this prevailing view, many of Chapman's patients expressed amazement that the Liverpool firefighter was able to provide professional diagnoses and perform miraculous healing procedures on them. Several claim they are alive today because of the words and deeds of Dr. Lang as he communicated through Chapman.

Dr. Fritz

One of the most prominent spirit surgeons in Brazil, José Arigó, began practicing in 1950. Arigó claimed that one day he had a vision of a bald spirit guide named Dr. Fritz who was dressed in white and working in a huge operating room with dozens of doctors and nurses. Arigó claims the spirit of Adolph Fritz then entered his body and began guiding his hands, helping him perform spirit surgery on numerous patients.

Arigó became famous throughout Brazil and was said to have removed a cancerous tumor from the lung of an important senator. However, the spirit surgeon was arrested several times for practicing medicine without a license before he died in a car accident in 1971. After Arigó's death, several other Brazilian healers claimed they, too, were guided by the spirit of Dr. Fritz.

George Chapman worked for free and did not seek fame. He regarded himself as a servant with the power to heal. However, according to Dr. Lang the only reason he performed the operations was to prove the existence of life after death. Healing the sick was a secondary mission.

CHAPTER 4

Electronic Communications

In 1988 psychic investigator James McClenon was investigating a 200-year-old haunted house in Durham, North Carolina. The residents of the home had experienced numerous frightening incidents traced to a poltergeist, including beds shaking violently and an apparition jumping out of a closet before disappearing into thin air. McClenon believed he could find the source of the problem by searching for electronic voice phenomena, or EVP. To do so, he ran his tape recorder in a silent room. When he was listening to the sounds on the tape later in the day, McClenon distinctly heard a male voice uttering nonsense phrases such as, "a quarter millions bucks!" "Shorty Short Stick," "Which side is the shingle on," and "Sorry Tink." While the voices were unusual and exciting to hear, McClenon writes that no "connection was discovered between these utterances and any other features of the case."[38]

Recording the Dead

The concept of recording EVP can be traced back to Thomas Edison, who became a renowned public figure after inventing the phonograph in 1877. Edison's list of inventions also includes the lightbulb, electric power distribution, and the movie camera. In 1920, when he was 73, Edison said he was working on a machine that would record messages from beyond the grave. In an October interview with *Scientific American*, Edison described why he was working on this idea:

> If our personality survives, then it is strictly logical or scientific to assume that it retains memory, intellect, other faculties, and knowledge that we acquire on this Earth. . . . If this reasoning be correct, then, if we can evolve an instrument so delicate as to be affected, or moved, or manipulated by our personality as it survives in the next life, such an instrument, when made available, ought to record something.[39]

Edison's interest in communicating with those in the afterlife was sparked by his friendship with William Crookes, a British scientist and paranormal investigator. Crookes was a collector of spirit photographs, and the images of alleged ghosts in the pictures convinced Edison that technology could be used to bridge the gap between this world and the next. It was said that Edison worked on an afterlife recording instrument until his death in 1931. While a popular magician of the day named Joseph Dunniger claimed to have seen such a device, no prototype or plans have ever been found.

Inventor Thomas Edison displays one of his inventions, the electric lightbulb, in his New Jersey laboratory. Edison thought it might be possible to record messages from the afterlife.

Electronic Voice Phenomena

The phrase "electronic voice phenomena" first came into use at the beginning of the electronic age when radio

engineers heard what seemed to be strange, unearthly voices barely audible beneath the static. Edison probably heard these mysterious noises while working on his various inventions. However, it was not until 28 years after his death that major experiments were conducted to isolate and decipher EVP.

In 1959 Swedish film producer and artist Friedrich Jurgenson was recording songbirds on his estate in Monnbo, Sweden. When he returned to his house to listen to the sounds on his reel-to-reel tape recorder, Jurgenson discovered more than birdsong. The tape also contained odd noises and the whispery voice of a man speaking in Norwegian, a language understood by Jurgenson. The strange voice was talking about the differences between the songs birds made during the day and those sung at night. Jurgenson later described the noises on his tape:

> I heard a noise, vibrating like a storm, where you could only remotely hear the chirping of the birds. My first thought was that maybe . . . [the tape recorder] had been damaged. In spite of this I switched on the machine again and let the tape roll. Again I heard this peculiar noise and the distant chirping. Then I heard a trumpet solo, a kind of a signal for attention. Stunned, I continued to listen when suddenly a man's voice began to speak in Norwegian. Even though the voice was quite low I could clearly hear and understand the words. The man spoke about "nightly bird voices" and I perceived a row of piping, splashing, and rattling sounds. Suddenly the choir of birds and the vibrating noise stopped. In the next moment the

Did You Know?
American photographer Attila von Szalay said he was able to record spirit voices on phonograph records in 1936.

chirping of a chaffinch was heard and you could hear [birds] singing at a distance—the machine was working perfectly![40]

As a filmmaker, Jurgenson understood the most up-to-date technology of the day. This led him to suspect that the tape recorder had somehow picked up transmissions from a local radio show. He called several stations in the area, but none were broadcasting programs about birdsong.

Mystified, Jurgenson set out to make recordings in different areas of his large estate. The new tape was startling, filled with EVP that included several voices. After repeated listening, Jurgenson discovered one of the voices was his deceased mother, who referred to him by a childhood nickname, "Little Friedel," that only she would know. Additional voices sounded like other dead relatives.

Voices from Space

Over the course of the next several years, Jurgenson continued to record voices on his estate and elsewhere. In 1964 he released his EVP tapes on a record called *Voices from Space*. The record attracted the attention of Latvian philosopher and psychologist Konstantin Raudive, who visited Jurgenson at his estate. Raudive made recordings

British scientist William Crookes (pictured) was also an investigator of paranormal events. His collection of ghost photographs may have influenced Thomas Edison's thoughts on a device for communicating with the dead.

that confirmed Jurgenson's findings, and the two men published their recording techniques in *Radio-Link with the Beyond*. The book, published in German and Swedish, was immensely popular in Europe and spawned an EVP movement in the late 1960s. Hundreds of engineers and amateur radio enthusiasts began conducting their own experiments, and many received similar results. Interestingly, news of the investigations reached the Vatican, the administrative center of the Catholic Church. And as EVP researcher Konstantinos writes in *Contact the Other Side*, the reaction of the church was unexpected: "[The] church didn't see any danger in the tapes. Rather than condemn the voices as some kind of heretical experiment, the church considered the voices a mystery controlled by the province of God, because the dead are in his kingdom and under his divine power."[41]

The concept of EVP soon spread to the United States, where it became a popular tool among paranormal researchers seeking to communicate with the other side. For example, paranormal investigator Katherine Ramsland often hunts ghosts with EVP. In an interview with journalist Suzy Hansen, Ramsland described the EVP recordings that she had made over the years:

> Sometimes [the voices] sound staticky, like they're having a hard time communicating. But you can tell male from female, oftentimes, and I've been able to tell whether they're young or old. The quality isn't as good as . . . talking on the phone—but definitely you can tell that there's personality. You can hear inflections. I've had some communications on my recorder that are really hard to understand, but you can certainly

Talking the Spirit Talk

Beginning in 1965 Latvian researcher Konstantin Raudive conducted extensive experiments with electronic voice phenomena (EVP). Raudive claims he was able to record the voices of dead Latvian writers and poets, along with those of his relatives and various close friends. According to Raudive, these voices had several common features that are also regularly heard on other EVP recordings:

1. The voice-entities speak very rapidly, in a mixture of languages, sometimes as many as five or six in one sentence.
2. They speak in a definite rhythm, which seems to be forced upon them by the means of communication they employ.
3. The rhythmic mode of speech imposes a shortened, telegram-style phrase or sentence.
4. Presumably arising from these restrictions, grammatical rules are frequently abandoned and neologisms [recently coined phrases] abound.

Konstantin Raudive, *Breakthrough: An Amazing Experiment in Electronic Communication with the Dead*. London: Colin Smythe, 1971, pp. 31–32.

hear that language is being used. They seem to have this quick window of opportunity to say something, but when they do, they say very provocative things. The one I liked the most said, "We keep busy."[42]

Broadcast Static

In order to record spirit communications, investigators like Ramsland follow basic techniques pioneered by Jurgenson and Raudive. After setting up a tape recorder with a high-quality microphone that can pick up a wide range of sounds, an investigator will try to achieve a very calm or trancelike state of mind using breathing techniques, meditation, or similar methods. In this condition a researcher can call out to dead friends, relatives, and even celebrities, asking them questions about any topic. Sessions are kept short, because a 15-minute tape needs to be analyzed repeatedly for hours. This allows investigators to pick out the soft, garbled voices that often speak in a very fast manner. After careful scrutiny of a tape, Raudive states, "the utterances become audible, the content clear and . . . identifiable to the human ear."[43]

Raudive perfected another EVP technique, called broadcast static recording, still in use today. To record spirit communications with this method, a tape recorder is connected to a radio tuned to static, the random crackling noise heard at the ends of the radio dial and between stations.

Those who believe in EVP say that broadcast static provides an easier way for the dead to talk. Instead of having to manifest physical voices that can be picked up by a microphone, spirits can use their energy to control the sound of the static, turning electronic noise into words. According to Konstantinos, "There is more sonic 'stuff' to work with in a noisy . . . signal [which] can be manipulated by a supernatural force—the mental force of the dead."[44]

Broadcast static recording is controversial. Skeptics say words heard in the crackling sounds are simply voices that "leak" onto the tape from established radio stations.

However, believers say the messages are not disc jockeys or popular songs, but personalized messages that could only come from the spirit world, such as the one heard by Konstantinos: "[I] can see you from the other side."[45]

Some EVP enthusiasts have found that the way to eliminate the possibility of interference from earthbound disc jockeys is to record white noise. This monotonous, static-like sound is produced by white noise generators or computer programs that create a tone used to help people relax. Sounds similar to white noise can also be created by natural forces, such as waves crashing on the beach, waterfalls, or even the wind blowing on a microphone. Whatever the source, white noise is said to work in a manner similar to broadcast static, providing a sound wave that can be manipulated into words by the dead.

An Ohio ghost hunter tries to record other-worldly com-munications known as electronic voice phenomena, or EVP. The quality of EVP recordings is often poor but ghost hunters believe they are neverthe-less real.

Instrumental Transcommunication

Searching for unearthly voices buried in a static signal is difficult work for most investigators. And the muddled results are easy for skeptics to criticize. Consequently, EVP investigators have moved beyond radios and tape recorders to obtain spirit communications with camcorders and TV sets.

Creating videos of ghosts requires more than pressing the record button on a camcorder. The camera needs to be hooked into the TV and pointed at the screen, which causes video feedback. Most people are familiar with audio feedback, the loud, piercing sound sometimes heard when a person is talking or singing into a microphone. Technically, feedback is created when an output signal returns to the input point, creating a feedback loop.

Paranormal investigators create video feedback to open what they call a "feedback loop doorway" to the dead. While the bright light produced by the feedback is painful to look at, people who point their camcorders at the TV screen can allegedly see dead friends, relatives, and strangers in the random video feedback.

In 1985 German psychic Klaus Schreiber was one of the first people to use the video feedback technique. Schreiber claimed to be receiving messages from Albert Einstein, Austrian actress Romy Schneider, and various departed family members, including two deceased wives and his daughter Karin. Some of the messages included instructions on how to adjust the video equipment to obtain a better signal from the other world. According to afterlife researcher Mike Pettigrew, the "result was a churning mist on the screen out of which the spirit faces would slowly form over a period of many frames."[46]

Since the video messages Schreiber received were not strictly voice phenomena, he coined the phrase "instrumental transcommunication," or ITC. This is now used by investigators when referring to spirit communication made through any sort of electronic device.

Schreiber died soon after his discovery, but according to some ITC investigators, the deceased psychic soon began appearing on their TVs. His messages confirmed the beliefs that EVP was indeed communication from beyond the grave.

Believers say the video camera works for spirit communications because those on the other side can manipulate electrons in the equipment to provide pictures and sound. As Konstantinos describes it: "This visual technique . . . is a powerful way to prove to yourself that your loved ones are indeed in a happy place. Whether you see them smiling or surrounded by beautiful scenery or both, your loved ones will communicate to you an immense wealth of information with each picture they transmit. . . . You're [seeing] into the afterlife!"[47]

Although microphones make it possible for everyone in the audience to hear a live concert, sometimes they create a screeching sound known as feedback. Feedback can disrupt a performance, but some paranormal investigators have tried using a similar type of feedback to open doorways to the dead.

Computer Connections

Camcorders have taken spirit communications into the digital age. And with the explosive growth of the Internet in the 1990s, it is not surprising that investigators began searching their hard drives for messages from the spirit world. As EVP and ITC researcher Michael Firman writes, "Forget about Ouija boards, séances and spiritual mediums. The way to communicate with the dead in the twenty-first century is through . . . computers and electronics [that] have revolutionized life on this planet."[48]

The computer connection with the dead began in 1980 when a West German researcher, Manfred Boden, began receiving a series of spontaneous messages splashed across his monitor. At first the missives appeared as letters, then sentences and paragraphs, allegedly sent by Boden's deceased friend.

Four years later an even more astounding dialogue began. Professor Kenneth Webster of Cheshire, England, started receiving computer messages from the spirit of an Englishman named Thomas Harden writing from the year 1546. At the time, the personal computer was in its infancy. PCs only had tiny 32-kilobyte memory chips—enough to hold a few pages of type. And modems and Internet connections were not available to the general public.

Webster did not even have a printer. But despite his archaic equipment, he received over 250 messages from Harden between 1984 and late 1985. The sixteenth-century ghost left messages on the computer screen, which he called a "light box," saying he was stuck in time. Some of the messages were written in a poetic style, while others were described as childlike nonsense or unreadable. However, some had a threatening tone. For example, Harden was apparently upset that Webster lived in his former home, leaving a message that translated, "You are a good person and you have a fantastic wife. But you live in my house. It was a big crime to steal my home."[49]

Harden allegedly wrote in an old English dialect and spent a great deal of time describing life as it was lived more than 400 years earlier: "This season I hath much to do, I hath to sow myne barly for myne ale, 'tis this that is myne craft and for whiche I am beste atte I fancy."[50]

Webster conducted extensive research and confirmed the messages conveyed by Harden about village life in the area were indeed based on fact. The professor later described the ghostly communication in the book *The Vertical Plane*.

Phone Calls from Beyond

Webster's messages from Harden were one-way communications from beyond the grave. But 3 years later 2 German researchers, Fritz Malkhoff and Adolf Homes, claimed to have conducted a 2-way conversation with their spirit friends. In 1988 Malkhoff and Homes set up a computer system whereby they typed short questions to the dead and left them on the screen. They said that 2 days later spirits answered the questions. Within a few years, Malkhoff and Homes said the spirits dispensed with the computer and began calling them on the telephone.

Homes and Malkhoff were among 16 ITC investigators who formed the organization INIT, or the International Network for Instrumental Transcommunication. When the researchers met in 1995, they discovered that phone calls from the dead were increasing rapidly among the INIT community. According to Pettigrew:

> Ethereal beings told us they were observing our efforts closely and would provide guidance and support. We began to experience unprecedented miracles in our research. Many of us

Did You Know?
The AAEVP organizes biweekly sessions called the Big Circle in which investigators conduct simultaneous EVP recording sessions all over the world to communicate with the dead.

received phone calls, usually from spirit friend Konstantin Raudive [who died in 1974]. Our ethereal friends told us that the greatest strides would be made by individuals from different countries who committed to work together in harmony with pure intentions.[51]

Pettigrew claims Raudive called him seven times and on one occasion they talked for 15 minutes. The dead EVP researcher assured Pettigrew that he was dedicated to advancing spirit communications and would continue to advise him from "the other side of the veil."[52] In addition to Raudive, INIT investigators said they received spirit phone calls from Friedrich Jurgenson, who died in 1987, as well as Klaus Schreiber, who passed away in 1988.

"Your Life Goes On"

With more than 1 billion people now using computers and the Internet, the number of ITC spirit communications has increased dramatically. Today hundreds of mediums and researchers have published Web pages with digital messages allegedly received from the dead. There are also dozens of EVP and ITC messages available for viewing on video sharing sites such as YouTube.

Some find it difficult to believe that the dead are speaking from beyond the grave on electronic instruments. However, believers think the soul is eternal and remains alive. According to Homes, when Jurgenson appeared on his TV in 1994, the deceased researcher affirmed this belief, saying: "Every being is a unity of spirit and body that cannot be separated on earth or in spirit. The only difference is the fact that the physical body disintegrates and in its place comes the astral body. Our message is to tell you that your life goes on."[53]

Searching for Proof

In April 1901 Duncan Macdougall, a surgeon and physician, was closely observing the patients at the Consumptives Home in Dorchester, Massachusetts. The Consumptives Home was a medical facility where consumptives, or those suffering from tuberculosis (TB), were taken to live out their final days. At the time, TB was fatal, but Macdougall was not striving to find a cure to save lives. Rather, he was waiting eagerly for patients to die.

Macdougall had been trying to prove the existence of the human soul since 1897. He firmly believed that if the soul existed, it must inhabit part of the human body. Macdougall wrote that personality and consciousness must "occupy space."[54] Attempting to prove this theory, Macdougall stalked the rooms of the sick and dying at the Consumptives Home. When a patient was near death, he or she was placed on a cot fixed to a specially built, highly accurate scale. If patients were lighter upon dying, it would prove that their soul had weight and therefore existed.

Macdougall describes how the death of one of his patients confirmed his beliefs: "At the end of three hours and forty minutes he expired and suddenly coincident with death the beam end [of the scale] dropped with an audible stroke. . . . The loss was ascertained to be three-fourths of an ounce."[55] Believing that the soul weighed three-fourths

Did You Know?
The word *parapsychology* was adopted to replace the term *psychical research* in the 1930s by J.B. Rhine, who believed the word described a more scientific approach to the study of the paranormal.

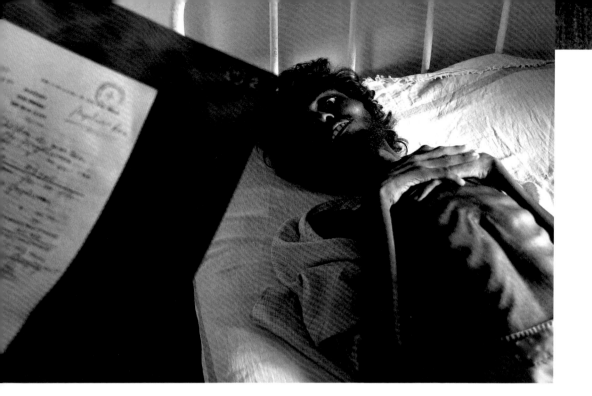

An emaciated tuberculosis patient awaits death in India. Physician Duncan Macdougall weighed tuberculosis patients immediately before and after death in hopes of finding a human soul. Spiritualists saw his work as possible proof of an afterlife.

of an ounce, Macdougall decided to describe it in metric measurements. He called it 21 grams because he believed it was easier for people to remember.

Macdougall's ghoulish experiments have little basis in scientific fact, since a body can lose 21 grams through loss of liquids after death. Whatever the case, the doctor's work was exciting to spiritualists who desperately wanted proof that the soul existed. To them it meant the afterlife was real and their efforts to communicate with the dead were anchored in reality.

Psychical Research

Macdougall was one of hundreds of scientists in the early twentieth century searching for scientific evidence of the afterlife. Others were trying to confirm the existence of ghosts and the accuracy of mediums, Ouija boards, and automatic writing and speech.

The movement to find scientific proof for paranormal phenomena began in the 1880s, when sensationalistic accounts of ghost sightings and séances began to filter in to British newspaper stories. There were so many people talking to the dead that William Barrett and Edmund Dawson Rogers founded the Society for Psychical Research (SPR) in London in 1882. Three years later, a similar organization, the American Society for Psychical Research (ASPR), was formed in the United States. The goal of the SPR and ASPR was to separate legitimate ghost-hunting activities from the fraudulent activities of many mediums.

The ASPR's headquarters in New York City remains open to researchers in the twenty-first century. Its library archives contain thousands of case records, trance drawings, spirit photographs, automatic writings, and other material dating back nearly 150 years.

Children Channel the Dead

In 1957 the research conducted by members of the ASPR caught the attention of Ian Stevenson, who was chair of the Department of Psychiatry at the University of Virginia. Stevenson had developed an interest in the paranormal during his childhood and decided to study the subject more intensively as a professor, writing: "I began to ask myself about the evidence for the unusual phenomena reported in the books I had read. It did not seem conclusive, but it also did not seem [unimportant]. So I read more about psychical research."[56] Stevenson began using the term *parapsychology* to describe his work. This term, which originated in the nineteenth century, defines a discipline that uses scientific methods to investigate paranormal

Shopkeepers play cards in Darbhanga, India, a city that became the focus of one of Ian Stevenson's investigations into past lives. One of Stevenson's interview subjects, a young girl, claimed she was murdered years earlier in a busy commercial district of Darbhanga.

phenomena such as life after death and psychic abilities.

Stevenson's interest in parapsychology led him to India, where he set up meetings with several dozen young children who claimed to remember past lives. In such cases, young children begin speaking convincingly about events that happened in distant towns many years before they were born. For example, Stevenson described a little girl named Kumkum Verma, aged three and a half. Kumkum claimed to have lived in the Urdu Bazar neighborhood of Darbhanga, a large city 25 miles (40km) from her small village. When Kumkum talked about her previous life, she spoke with an accent and employed expressions that were only used by people of Urdu Bazar.

Kumkum's father was a respected author and landowner but did not know anyone in Urdu Bazar, a commercial district populated by businesspeople, artisans, and craftspeople. In a book about Stevenson's research, *Life Before Life*, Kumkum's unusual recall is described:

> Kumkum asked her family to call her Sunnary, which means beautiful, and made many statements about the previous life. Her aunt made notes. . . . The extracts listed eighteen statements that Kumkum made that all proved to be correct for the previous personality, including . . . her son's name and the fact that he worked with a hammer, her grandson's name, the name of the town where her father lived, the location of his home near mango orchards, and the presence of a pond at her house. She had correctly stated that she had an iron safe at her house, a sword hanging near her cot, and a snake near the safe to which she fed milk.[57]

After doing extensive research in Urdu Bazar, Kumkum's father confirmed his daughter's story. There was indeed a person named Sunnary who died five years before Kumkum was born. Sunnary's father lived near mango orchards, and her son worked with a hammer as a blacksmith. The most interesting aspect, however, provided a reason why Sunnary might have been communicating through the little girl. Kumkum said that Sunnary died after being poisoned by her stepson's wife in a dispute over a large sum of money. Stevenson speculated that the dead woman was talking through Kumkum in order to alert authorities to her murder.

Survival of Personality After Death

After publishing an article about Kumkum and similar children, Stevenson was contacted by Chester F. Carlson, who was intensely interested in reincarnation and afterlife communications. Carlson was the inventor of xerography, or photocopying, and offered to fund Stevenson's research. With Carlson's help, Stevenson widened his field of study, applying scientific methods to research apparitions, mediums, and spirit photography.

Carlson died in 1968 but bequeathed $1 million to the University of Virginia in his will so Stevenson could continue studying paranormal phenomena. This sum allowed Stevenson to form the Division of Perceptual Studies (DOPS) as a unit of the Department of Psychiatric Medicine at the university. In the following years the dozen or so faculty members in the department gained international fame for their research into what Stevenson called the "survival of personality after death."[58]

While incredible advances have been made in medicine, computers, and other fields in recent decades, even the most diligent researchers have not been able to prove the existence of ghosts or the afterlife. For example, before his own death in February 2007, Stevenson recorded over 2,500 fascinating cases concerning alleged apparition sightings, after-death communications, deathbed visions of the afterlife, and children with past-life experiences. And his colleagues in the department have cataloged thousands of additional cases. However, all of this work only provides a basis for theory and speculation, not scientific proof of life after death.

Perception at PEAR

The lack of such scientific breakthroughs is behind the demise of one of the most respected parapsychology departments in the United States. In 2007 the Princeton Engineering Anomalies Research (PEAR) laboratory closed its doors after 27 years of study. As part of Princeton University's School of Engineering and Applied Science, PEAR conducted research into the link between human consciousness and its ability to affect the physical world.

Researchers at PEAR consisted of highly respected engineers, psychologists, and physicists. One major field of study concerned remote viewing, also called remote perception or clairvoyance. This is the technique practiced by mediums who claim to use psychic powers to perceive people, places, and actions that are not visible to others. Remote viewing allows mediums to see spirits, channel ghosts, and read minds. It also allows them to visualize events in the past, in the future, or taking place at distant locations in the present.

PEAR conducted 653 remote perception experiments over the course of 25 years. These were conducted with an observer, called an agent, stationed at a remote location, such as Loch Ness in Scotland. The viewer, called a percipient, was asked to describe the scene as the agent saw it. Although the percipient was situated at Princeton, thousands of miles away in New Jersey, according to the PEAR Web site, "even casual comparison of the agent and percipient [descriptions] produced in this body of experiments reveals striking [similarities] . . . well beyond any chance expectations."[59]

Did You Know?
Arthur Balfour, the prime minister of Great Britain from 1902 to 1905, also served as president of the Society for Psychical Research.

Spirit Guides, Angels, and Other-Worldly Entities

The PEAR experiments seemed to prove that mediums had paranormal powers that allowed them to see the unseen. However, funding was halted for the PEAR program, and it folded without providing proof of psychic powers and spirits. Studies continued, however, at the VERITAS Research Program in the Department of Psychology at the University of Arizona in Tucson. This program was created in 2000 by Gary E. Schwartz, a professor of psychology, medicine, neurology, psychiatry, and surgery. The primary mission of VERITAS was to test the theory that the consciousness, personality, or identity survives physical death and speaks to the living. As Schwartz describes it:

> The purpose of this study is to investigate the experiences of people who claim to channel or communicate with Deceased People, Spirit Guides, Angels, Other-Worldly Entities/Extraterrestrials, and/or a Universal Intelligence/God. The ultimate objective is to investigate if these communications can be validated under controlled conditions.[60]

The motto of the VERITAS program is "If it is real, it will be revealed. If it is fake, we'll find the mistake."[61] Following this concept, VERITAS researchers screened dozens of mediums to participate in its challenging study. Those who truly exhibited psychic abilities were selected for research. VERITAS subjects submitted to detailed personality and psychological tests. They also conducted "blind" readings (for anonymous subjects) in tests conducted in person and by e-mail and telephone. In addition, the mediums took courses called mediumship research training,

Scoring Mediums

In 2005 VERITAS researchers conducted extensive scientific tests on mediums and their ability to communicate with the dead. In order to judge the abilities of the mediums, each one was awarded a score based on his or her skills. While some mediums scored well, others did not, but researchers concluded there was evidence of "survival of consciousness, or the continued existence, separate from the body, of an individual's consciousness or personality after physical death."

The scoring method was as follows:

6: Excellent reading, including strong aspects of communication, and with essentially no incorrect information.

5: Good reading with relatively little incorrect information.

4: Good reading with some incorrect information.

3: Mixture of correct and incorrect information, but enough correct information to indicate that communication with the deceased occurred.

2: Some correct information, but not enough to suggest beyond chance that communication occurred.

1: Little correct information or communication.

0: No correct information or communication.

Julie Beischel and Gary E. Schwartz, "Anomalous Information Reception by Research Mediums Demonstrated Using a Novel Triple-Blind Protocol," *Explore*, January/February 2007, p. 25.

human research training, and grief training to improve their work with clients.

Those who have completed the VERITAS program call themselves integrative research mediums (IRMs). IRMs are given a certificate, a seal of approval, that can be displayed on Web sites and office walls. According to certified medium Joanne Gerber, IRMs are "committed to being Honest, Open, Ethical, Responsible, Compassionate, Respectful, Humble, and Gracious. They value Truth, Science, Ethics, Responsibility, Compassion, Healing, Health, Evolution, and Growth."[62]

Gerber calls herself a psychic medium. She works with clients who want to connect with someone who has died. Gerber describes her channeling technique on her Web site:

> I will be connecting to those who have passed and who are able to connect with you at the time of the reading. . . . Besides describing what the person may have looked like here on the earth plane, I will also sense their individual personality, and ask them for as many details as possible, such as birthday and anniversary dates, dates of passing, names, and maybe what kind of work they did here on the earth plane. . . . My intention . . . is to work with those in the spirit world, asking for as much validation as possible so that it will leave no doubt in your mind that your loved one, or loved ones, have communicated with you from the spirit world.[63]

In 2008 VERITAS codirector Julie Beischel founded the Windbridge Institute for Applied Research in Human

Did You Know?

When psychiatrist Jim Tucker studied children who remember previous lives, he found that 75 percent had distinct memories of their deaths.

Potential. At Windbridge, scientists continue to perform afterlife and mediumship research, certifying IRMs with the same program used at VERITAS.

The Survivalists

Not all afterlife research is conducted at public institutions like the University of Arizona. For example, the Campaign for Philosophical Freedom (CPF) is a private institution sponsored by donations and grants. According to the organization's Web site: "Scientific proof of survival after death has existed for over a century. The CPF is working to increase public awareness of the existence of scientific proof that we all survive the death of our physical bodies—irrespective of religious beliefs."[64]

The CPF was founded in Bristol, England, by paranormal investigator and author Michael Roll. Members of the organization reject spiritualism because they think it is too much like a religion in which believers attend church and accept belief in the afterlife on faith alone. As Roll writes, "Many Spiritualists . . . have been fighting . . . to block the scientific backup for what mediums have been saying—that our loved ones are not dead."[65]

Rejecting spiritualism, members of the CPF call themselves survivalists because they think people survive after their bodies have died. Survivalist J.J. Snyder says that proof of the afterlife has been found by those studying mathematics and physics. According to Snyder:

> [Scientists] now furnish verification for . . . what has been previously known as "psychic phenomena." These experiments . . . conducted by various researchers from the late nineteenth century down to the present day . . . have a common thread. Each

Did You Know?
According to research conducted by Windbridge Institute, there is substantial scientific evidence to support the accuracy of telephone readings by mediums.

features repeated appearances by, and communication with, entities from the next level of existence who have experienced the event known as death, and yet maintain consciousness, remain articulate, and sometimes become visible on this physical level. At times these visitors from [other] realms can be touched, felt, and even held tightly by incarnate humans.[66]

These entities can be summoned by mediums or called forth by the strong emotions of the living. Survivalists contend that appearances by the dead are governed by natural physical laws based on the behavior of electrons, protons, neutrons, and other subatomic particles.

No Scientific Justification

Despite the efforts by Roll and researchers at public institutions, there is great skepticism among mainstream scientists concerning life-after-death phenomena. In 1988 the U.S. National Academy of Sciences addressed the issue, writing that there is "no scientific justification from research conducted over a period of 130 years for the existence of parapsychological phenomena."[67]

Despite such conclusions some will undoubtedly continue to listen for communications from the dead. Many people take comfort from the idea that they may hear soothing words from a loved one who has died. Whether the words are actually projected from the afterlife or simply a figment of the imagination, they often provide a healing balm for the soul and give survivors a reason to go on living another day.

Source Notes

Introduction: Spirits and Spiritualism

1. Quoted in Jean H. Baker, *Mary Todd Lincoln: A Biography.* New York: Norton, 1987, p. 220.
2. Baker, *Mary Todd Lincoln*, p. 218.
3. Robert T. Carroll, "Subjective Validation," The Skeptic's Dictionary. http://skepdic.com.
4. Bob Olson, "The Grief and Belief Connection," Grief and Belief. http://griefandbelief.com.

Chapter 1: A Medium in the Middle

5. Quoted in Bob Olson, "Profile on Rita Berkowitz, Spirit Artist," Best Psychic Mediums, January 24, 2009. www.bestpsychicmediums.com.
6. Barbara Weisberg, *Talking to the Dead.* San Francisco: HarperCollins, 2004, pp. 99–100.
7. Quoted in Frank Podmoer, *Mediums of the 19th Century*, vol. 2. New Hyde Park, NY: University, 1963, p. 48.
8. Quoted in Troy Taylor, "The Mystery of Patience Worth," American Hauntings. www.prairieghosts.com.
9. Taylor, "The Mystery of Patience Worth."
10. Alleee and Franc, "So, You Wanna Be a Psychic?" Insolitology. www.insolitology.com.
11. Alleee and Franc, "So, You Wanna Be a Psychic?"

Chapter 2: Speaking with Spooks

12. Harry Price, *The Most Haunted House in England.* London: Longmans, Green, 1990, p. 194.
13. Troy Taylor, "Borley Rectory: The History of 'The Most Haunted House in England,'" American Hauntings. www.prairieghosts.com.
14. Raymond Bayless, *The Enigma of the Poltergeist.* West Nyack, NY: Parker, 1967, p. 79.
15. Colin Wilson, *Poltergeist! A Study in Destructive Haunting.* St. Paul, MN: Llewellyn, 1993, pp. 110–11.
16. Quoted in Hans Holzer, *Ghosts: True Encounters with the World Beyond.* New York: Black Dog & Leventhal, 1997, p. 672.
17. Quoted in Holzer, *Ghosts*, p. 674.
18. Quoted in Holzer, *Ghosts*, p. 675.
19. Quoted in Holzer, *Ghosts*, p. 688.
20. Holzer, *Ghosts*, p. 689.

Chapter 3: Spirit Guides

21. Sylvia Browne, *The Other Side and Back*. New York: Dutton, 1999, pp. 20–21.
22. Native American Drumming Circle, "Drumming and Dancing with Spirit Circle." http://nativeamericanmeetup. com.
23. Quoted in Stephen C. Wehmeyer, "Indians at the Door: Power and Placement on New Orleans Spiritual Church Altars," *Western Folklore*, Winter 2007, p. 5.
24. John J. Guthrie Jr., Phillip Charles Lucas, and Gary Monroe, eds., *Cassadaga: The South's Oldest Spiritualist Community*. Gainesville: University Press of Florida, 2000, p. 67.
25. Orrin Lewis, "Seeking Native American Spirituality: Read This First!" Native Languages of the Americas. www. native-languages.org.
26. Weisberg, *Talking to the Dead*, p. 144.
27. Willow Sibert, "Psychic Readings and Channeling with Willow," Channeling with Willow. http:// channelingwithwillow.com.
28. Rita S. Berkowitz and Deborah S. Romaine, *The Complete Idiot's Guide to Communicating with Spirits*. Indianapolis: Alpha, 2003, p. 9.
29. Christopher Penczak, *Spirit Allies*. Boston: Weiser, 2002, p. 84.
30. Berkowitz and Romaine, *The Complete Idiot's Guide to Communicating with Spirits*, p. 12.
31. Browne, *The Other Side and Back*, p. 107.
32. Rosemary Altea, *Proud Spirit*. New York: William Morrow, 1997, p. 106.
33. Quoted in Fortune City, "The Mediumship of George Chapman." www.fortunecity.com.
34. Quoted in George Chapman, *Surgeon from Another World*. London: Psychic, 1978, pp. 28–29.
35. Quoted in Chapman, *Surgeon from Another World*, p. 41.
36. *Daily Telegraph*, "George Chapman," August 12, 2006. www.telegraph.co.uk.
37. Quoted in *New York Times*, "F.T.C. Curtails the Promotion of All Psychic Surgery Tours," October 25, 1975. http://select.nytimes.com.

Chapter 4: Electronic Communications

38. Quoted in James Houran and Rense Lange, eds., *Hauntings and Poltergeists*. Jefferson, NC: McFarland, 2001, p. 72.
39. Quoted in Joseph R. Tremonti, "Electronic Visualization Laboratory," University of Illinois at Chicago, July 2002. www.evl.uic.edu.
40. Quoted in Tremonti, "Electronic Visualization Laboratory."
41. Konstantinos, *Contact the Other Side*. St. Paul, MN: Llewellyn, 2001, p. 59.
42. Quoted on Suzy Hansen, "Ghost Writer," *Salon*, October 31, 2001, www.salon.com.
43. Konstantin Raudive, *Breakthrough: An Amazing Experiment in Electronic Communication with the Dead*. London: Colin Smythe, 1971, p. 21.
44. Konstantinos, *Contact the Other Side*, p. 90.
45. Quoted in Konstantinos, *Contact the Other Side*, p. 92.
46. Mike Pettigrew, "A Short History of EVP and ITC," The Institute for Afterlife Research. www.mikepettigrew.com.

47. Konstantinos, *Contact the Other Side*, p. 118.

48. Michael Firman, "The Dead Do Speak . . . and Michael Firman Listens!" Haunted America Tours, February 10, 2009. www.hauntedamericatours. com.

49. Quoted in Pettigrew, "A Short History of EVP and ITC."

50. Quoted in Dancin' Hamster, "The Vertical Plane," Unexplained Mysteries Discussions Forum, December 14, 2003. www.unexplained-mysteries. com.

51. Pettigrew, "A Short History of EVP and ITC."

52. Quoted in Pettigrew, "A Short History of EVP and ITC."

53. Quoted in Pettigrew, "A Short History of EVP and ITC."

Chapter 5: Searching for Proof

54. Quoted in Mary Roach, *Spook: Science Tackles the Afterlife*. New York: Norton, 2005, p. 80.

55. Quoted in Snopes, "Soul Man," July 17, 2007. www.snopes.com.

56. Ian Stevenson, "Half a Career with the Paranormal," *Journal of Scientific Exploration*, October 2006. www. healthsystem.virginia.edu.

57. Jim B. Tucker, "The Case of Kumkum Verma," *Life Before Life*. http://lifebefore life.com.

58. Quoted in Lee Graves, "Altered States," *University of Virginia Magazine*, Summer 2007. www.uvamagazine. org.

59. Princeton Engineering Anomalies Research, "II. Remote Perception." www.princeton.edu.

60. Quoted in University of Arizona, "The SOPHIA Project." http://lach. web.arizona.edu.

61. Quoted in University of Arizona, "The VERITAS Research Program." http:// veritas.arizona.edu.

62. Joanne Gerber, "Veritas Research Program." www.joannegerber.com.

63. Gerber, "Veritas Research Program."

64. Michael Roll, "About the Campaign for Philosophical Freedom," The Campaign for Philosophical Freedom. www.cfpf.org.uk.

65. Michael Roll, "The Scientific Proof of Survival After Death (Part 2)," The Campaign for Philosophical Freedom. www.cfpf.org.uk.

66. J.J. Snyder, "Science Confirms Survival," The Campaign for Philosophical Freedom. www.cfpf.org. uk.

67. Quoted in Paul H. Smith, *Reading the Enemy's Mind*. New York: Forge, 2005, p. 372.

For Further Research

Books

Jeff Belanger, *Who's Haunting the White House? The President's Mansion and the Ghosts Who Live There*. New York: Sterling, 2008.

Concetta Bertoldi, *Do Dead People Watch You Shower? And Other Questions You've Been All but Dying to Ask a Medium*. New York: HarperCollins, 2008.

Raymond Buckland, *The Spirit Book: The Encyclopedia of Clairvoyance, Channeling, and Spirit Communication*. Canton, MI: Visible Ink, 2006.

Karen Miller, *Paranormal Phenomena*. Detroit: Greenhaven, 2008.

Michael Teitelbaum, *Ghosts and Real-Life Ghost Hunters*. New York: Franklin Watts, 2008.

Eugene Yelchin, *Ghost Files: The Haunting Truth for Those Who Are Very Practical About Identifying, Documenting, and Classifying Apparitions, Ghosts, and Spirits from Early Men to Our Time; or, How to See a Ghost When You Much Prefer to Look Away and If You're Very Good, How to Make Contact*. New York: Harper Collins, 2008.

Internet Source

Alleee and Franc, "So, You Wanna Be a Psychic?" Insolitology. www.insolitology.com/rationally/edward.htm.

Web Sites

American Association of Electronic Voice Phenomena (www.aaevp.com). This site is run by people who are interested in electronic voice phenomena (EVP) and instrumental transcommunication (ITC). The Web site offers techniques for experimenting with EVP and ITC and has many examples of the phenomena, including voice recordings, photos, and videos said to be messages from the dead.

American Hauntings (www.prairieghosts.com). This Web site bills itself as the "Historic and Haunted Guide to the Supernatural" and contains extensive links to ghost stories, haunted houses, spirit photography, ghost hunting, and other subjects.

Do You Believe? A Ghostly Gallery, The American Museum of Photography (www.photographymuseum.com/believe1.html). This site contains many fascinating examples of spirit photography and the stories behind the images. Some pictures are obviously fake and others mysteriously haunting.

Haunted America Tours (www.hauntedamericatours.com). A Web site dedicated to ghosts and haunted houses. The site features dozens of articles about ghost hunting, spirit communications, séances, and electronic voice phenomena featuring audio samples of people talking from beyond the grave.

Medium, *The Skeptic's Dictionary* (http://skepdic.com/medium.html). This site exposes the tricks popular mediums use to fool people into thinking there is communication with the dead. Links on the site lead to articles that debunk ghosts, haunted houses, poltergeists, mediums, electronic voice phenomena, and other paranormal beliefs.

National Spiritualist Association of Churches (www.nsac.org). This Web site represents Spiritualist churches throughout the United States and provides dozens of free documents with information about Spiritualist beliefs.

Index